TOY INSTRUMENTS

LES ARTS DECORATIFS MUSEUM IN PARIS, MUSIQUE EN JOUETS EXPOSITION, 2009.
PHOTOGRAPHY: LUC BOEGLY

TOY INSTRUMENTS

DESIGN, NOSTALGIA, MUSIC
BY ERIC SCHNEIDER

MARK BATTY PUBLISHER ◣ NEW YORK

This book is dedicated to my mother and to my life's best inspiration—my daughter Jeanne.

I would like to thank the following people who have made this book possible: Jaro Gielens (who created www.miniorgan.com in order to communicate with people all over the world); Hiromichi Oohashi (who helped me find rare objects); Chris Garland, Brit Leissler, Celeste Najt and Max Neutra (who always believed in me as an artist).

I would also like to thank all the people from around world who sent wonderful emails or sold their toys to me. Last but not least, I would like to thank a huge online auction house—you made me addictive, but now I am famous and clean!

TABLE OF CONTENTS

A FEW WORDS ABOUT SMALL TOYS

Eric Schneider
Cologne, Germany, 2009

When people look at my shelves filled with over 250 shiny boxes of toy instruments it is easy for me to visualize a question mark floating above their heads. And then comes the inevitable question: Why?

It was Christmas 1979 or 1980. I was a young and strange schoolboy who had been infected by a mass of cool toy commercials on TV. A funny, mellow bearded guy named Bill Ramsey appeared on screen, playing a little machine that made a squeaky sound: The Stylophone! I was thrilled; I needed it I prayed for it. I put it on my Christmas list.

Later in life I learned that my mother had tried to buy it, but a shop clerk sold her something "much better for a kid"—the Concept 2000 Lite'n Learn. So instead of the small, sleek sophisticated organ I got a huge red soft rounded one with keys so big an elephant could have played it. I tortured my family with that monstrosity well into the New Year—but my Stylophone prayers remained unanswered.

Twenty years later I found an old computer magazine at a flea market and saw a little review of the Lite'n Learn. I was very surprised that such a cheap plastic toy got a "review." I started hunting around for the toy. While searching for it I passed over 250 other little sad machines and bought them. I wasn't able to resist, because I learned over the years that electronic musical toys from the 50s to the 90s are definitely the coolest topic in universe—believe me!

Electronic musical toys are the expression of our deepest dreams. They activate your personal creativity (even if you don't think you possess it). The sound is often horrible but always impressive. They offer strange learning concepts and surfaces with lots of knobs and sliders. They are pure fun, even when it is just for a minute. They have beautiful boxes with great art. Adorned with bizarre color schemes, always-happy families and boys and girls immune to gender disharmony, the toys and the packaging create a Shangri-La sheen, albeit one that is out of tune. They never crash! What else gives you so much?

This book contains the best of the best. Maybe you're old enough to find your own Christmas-Trauma or you're young enough to see that the good old times were really the better times.

SERIOUS PLAY

Paul D. Miller aka DJ Spooky that Subliminal Kid

Reality is that which, when you stop believing in it, doesn't go away.

Philip K. Dick, "How to Build a Universe That Doesn't Fall Apart Two Days Later," 1978

We live in an era where almost everything we do online is tracked one way or another: think collaborative filtering, link-track, number of downloads per file, etc. and you can see that there's an exponential explosion of what it means to interact with information. When people browse online, they're playing with icons, links and, above all, what some economists like to call the "attention economy"—the online world has evolved straight out of the realm of play when the objects around were still "solid" and made of things we could actually feel and hold.

What does this have to do with Eric Schneider's obsessive-compulsive collection of toy musical instruments? One word: everything.

Where pop culture, education and entertainment collide, who is there to organize the pieces? Is there a rhyme of reason to the way we look at and interact with the toys of our childhood? To design a puzzle, board game, playing cards or a musical keyboard—these are acts of sheer brilliance, mediated by the simplicity of user friendliness. That idea is at the heart of this book.

The writer Philip K. Dick liked to use games as a way of teaching us about the perils of science gone wild. Indeed, a lot of his characters were toys. Think of the titles to his stories like "War Game," "The Days of Perky Pat," "The Little Black Box," "A Game of Unchance" and you can see a thread that leads directly to some of the biggest movies of the last several decades: *Blade Runner, Running Man, Minority Report*. Dick was a visionary who thought that play and toys conditioned almost all aspects of everyday life. Did

you dig toy instruments as a kid? Do you use them today? Which of these toys appeal to you most, and why?

This question is a central issue of our "App Store" dominated world. Why do so many people download apps and games, play with them on their screens, use them to mediate everyday life? It's simple: because they are an essential part of the way we live. Games teach almost everything.

Guitar Hero, customized video game avatars, Wii, *Second Life, Vice City*…they're all games that mirror, in one way or another, the aspirations of the players. So too with the musical toys that Schneider has collected in this wonderful anthology.

There's something about the late twentieth century world of audio instruments that comprises Schneider's collection, which rings even more resonant with today's hyper-realist world of artists like Jeff Koons and philosophers like Jean Baudrillard, but that's a different essay. The essential thing is this: people play games in a way that is becoming more and more abstract, and that's cool. I just wish that they could see the toy instruments in this book to get a better idea of why the bleeps, trills and chimes they're hearing out of the video games, cell phone ring tones and web-alerts sound interesting—it's because they already have heard the sounds before, coming out of the objects that surrounded us in our childhood.

What makes the connection between life and its mirrored after effects? If you look at writers like William Gibson and Bruce Sterling, who use web-based "realism" as an inverted mirror of the things that hold together modern digital life and its near future, these musical instruments seem even more like signposts to the ongoing digitization of every aspect of modern life. Indeed, echoing through the halls of Google is the simple, but deeply reflective phrase: Everything that can be digital, will be.

Let's look at a game like Snakes and Ladders: any version of Snakes and Ladders can be represented exactly as a Markov chain, since from any square the odds of moving to any other square are fixed and independent of any previous game history. Got the math? No? Don't worry—your average kid doesn't either. That's kind of the point. In fact, the game was used to teach kids in India about intuitive mathematics, and the ideals of reincarnation.

The game was played throughout ancient India under the name of "Moksha Patamu," the earliest version dates back to 16th century and was eventually called "Leela"— "the game of knowledge." The game was meant to reflect Hindu consciousness around everyday life. Impressed by the ideals behind the game, a newer version was introduced in Victorian England in 1892 as "Chutes and Ladders," or the even more popular name "Snakes and Ladders," and from there it became one of the most popular games of the last two centuries. It was all about abstraction—here's a brief plot summary: The player's progress is dictated by the fall of a dice corresponding to the forces of karma. The seven planes through which the player must pass before she or he reaches the eighth plane—the plane beyond all planes—are the seven chakras. Right?

Leela is not merely an entertainment but a serious method of understanding the phenomenal world of Maya (Illusion), and the spiritual nature of our individual self that leads us to the journey toward liberation—or getting to the "next level." If you think about the rise of the instruments that abound in the collection you hold in your hands, they represent some accidental borrowings as well.

I'll give you another example: one of my favorite composers, Raymond Scott, created computers to make music. They didn't have computers back in the mid 1940s but that didn't stop him. He invented what he needed, and kept going. Over the course of his 50-year career, he made stuff that was used for jingles (he did the first electronic music for TV commercials for example), the score for uncountable TV shows and, above all, his music was used for cartoons, bumping next to characters like Daffy Duck, Bugs Bunny, Road Runner and eventually was adapted to the "Looney Tunes" theme. He even worked with Motown's Berry Gordy, trying to create an electronic funk machine that would replace Motown's famous in-house rhythm bands. Needless to say, nothing came out of that. Anyway, you've heard his music, but I bet you didn't know his name. You'll see some instruments in this collection that look like they could have come from his labs, and that's a good thing. How many of you know who designed the objects around us? How many of us care?

Think of how sound instruments guided our perceptions—anyone who has developed games can see that following a few basic tenets that can sound deceptively simple, makes the whole situation worthwhile.

For starters, by way of thinking like amazing visionaries such as Bob Moog, every player should be involved in every turn—even if just by asking a question or moving a game piece—to maximize interaction and to stave off boredom. Make an instrument that can be almost any synthesized sound, and roll with it. Stuff like that is what drove so much American innovation in the 20th century. I think of the material that Eric Schneider has compiled as a kind of "object" time machine, reaching back to the heart of what electronic music represented when it was new. I hope you enjoy the material that he's collected. Like we say in hip-hop, it represents some serious "diggin' in the crates."

KLING KLONG

Mechanical & Electro-Mechanical

Manufacturer: UNKNOWN
Name: BABY PIANO
Date, Place: 1960, JAPAN

A boy dreams of being an astronaut but he ends up making wooden toy pianos. Here is the inspiring result of such a dream deferred.

Bugs Bunny
Jelly Roll
Player Piano

© 1978 WARNER BROS. INC.

TOMATICALLY

THE KEYS

$20

Manufacturer: SEARS
Name: BUGS BUNNY PLAYER PIANO
Date, Place: 1978, HONG KONG

Three minutes of these monotonic detuned chords and you'll
jump like Bugs Bunny.

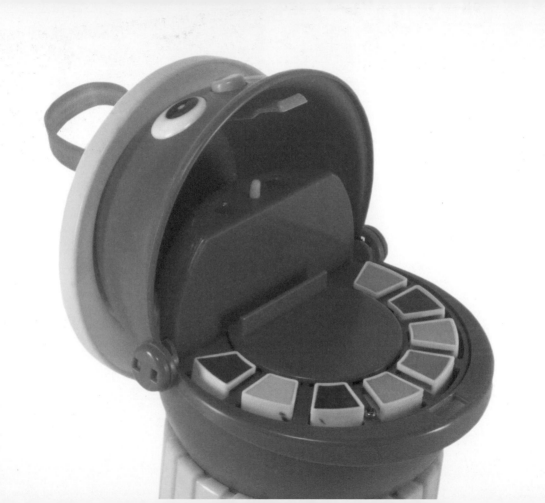

Manufacturer: A CHILD GUIDANCE TOY
Name: MELODY MIKE
Date, Place: UNKNOWN, HONG KONG

Don't brush your teeth regularly? Just play with Melody Mike and every inflamed nerve in your jaw will drive you to tears—and better oral hygiene.

バンダイ「ミュージックシリーズ」には、いろいろな楽器があります。
おこさまの年令・興味にあわせておかいもとめください。

リズムオルガン

製品には万全を期しておりますが、万一不都合な点がございましたら、製造元・サンリード工業迄、御問い

クラリネット

トランペット

サキソフォン

フレンドオルガン

フレンド

株式
会社 バンダイ
発売元 BANDAI
東京都台東区駒形2丁目5番4号

発売元 SUN サンリード工業株式会社
東京都荒川郵便局私書箱19号

ST
玩具安全基準合格
MIB92001
(社)日本玩具協会

ください。

Manufacturer: BANDAI
Name: FURENDO ORUGAN
Date, Place: UNKNOWN, JAPAN

I now know why Japanese people like childish cuteness so much—
to make every non-Japanese person happy. *Domo arigato!*

PIONEER ELECTRONICA

50s and 60s Toy Organs

1954's TOY SENSATION

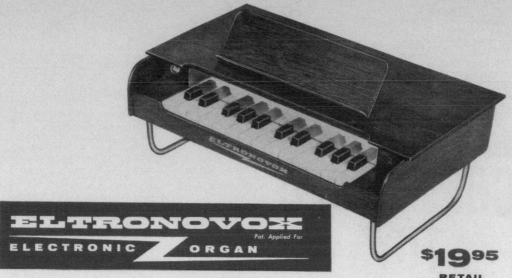

ELTRONOVOX
Pat. Applied For

ELECTRONIC **Z** ORGAN

$**19**⁹⁵

RETAIL
$21.95 west
of the Rockies

Amazing! Thrilling! Educational!

THE TONE OF AN ORGAN
FOR THE PRICE OF A TOY!

PLAYS THROUGH YOUR OWN RADIO WITHOUT CONNECTIONS! No wires
or plug-ins of any kind, transmits through any AM receiver—

TOY INSTRUMENTS PIONEER ELECTRONICA

Manufacturer: ASAHI
Name: ELECTRONIC ORGAN
Date, Place: 1959, JAPAN

Hurray! You don't need to go to church anymore! The rich cathedralic organ tones emanating from the loudspeaker surrounded by a reverb spring, sounds as if God is playing this little toy.

GENERAL ⓖⓔ ELECTRIC

1 **+1** 2

LOUD

ON   ON   HORN
                        BRASS
OFF   OFF   REED
                        FLUTE

                SOFT

POWER VIBRATO   VOL   VOICE

Manufacturer: GENERAL ELECTRIC
Name: TOTE-A-TUNE
Date, Place: 1971, USA

The era of sitting at a campfire, playing guitar and singing good ol' cowboy songs is definitely over. With Tote-a-Tune you sit in a starship and sing with Martians.

THE ONE AND ONLY

Stylophone & Clones

Album de films et comedies musicales

COMMENT APPRENDRE FACILEMENT A JOUER PAR NUMEROS

Manufacturer: DUBREQ
Name: STYLOPHONE
Date, Place: 1967, UK

Rolf Harris represents the toy's target demographic: bearded weirdos who'll never grow up.

TOY INSTRUMENTS THE ONE AND ONLY

PHOTO CONTROL

BATTERY
ELIMINATOR

Manufacturer: DUBREQ
Name: SUPER STYLOPHONE
Date, Place: ????, UK

This is definitely made for Big Players—a perfect present for your boss.

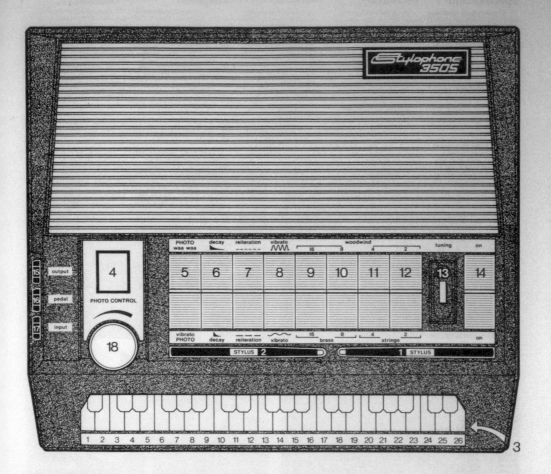

Stylophone gains ground in pop market

Previously aimed at the older age group, the Stylophone, a battery-operated transistorised pocket organ played with a stylus, has rapidly been gaining acceptance in the pop music field, particularly since its introduction to the Hit Parade via David Bowie's *Space Oddity*. The instrument is completely self-contained, and can be used on its own without external amplification, but it may, if required, be connected to a standard amplifier, as demonstrated by Diane Stewart with the Graham Bond Initiation.

The Stylophone has a 20-note keyboard laid out like a piano keyboard, with the additional facility of a back-mounted screw control for altering the pitch to accompany a record or another instrument. To play, the instrument is switched on and adjusted to either flat or vibrato tone, and a stylus is slid along the keyboard to produce the required note. Other tone variations may be achieved by manipulating the hand over the speaker grille, and this also acts as a volume control.

Costing £8 18s. 6d., the Stylophone may be obtained from most music shops or direct from the makers, Dubreq Studios Ltd., 15 Cricklewood Broadway, London NW2.

Charity pop concert

SHELTER, the National Campaign for the Homeless, are organising a charity pop concert at the Royal Albert Hall on December 19. Among the groups appearing are Family, whose single *No Mule's Fool* entered the charts this month and Sam Apple Pie, the East London group recently signed up by NEMS. Tickets are available from the Albert Hall box office at 8s. to 30s.

"Give the North a chance"

Alan Hull, 24 year old Newcastle folk singer/songwriter, feels very strongly that Northern artists don't get a fair crack at the whip. He would especially like to push various musicians from the Newcastle Arts Centre, of which he is an organiser. With his manager Alan has formed his own promotion company, and has plans to

Alan Hull

start his own record company.

finished recording his first single for Transatlantic, at Trident Studios in Wardour Street, which is surprisingly an out and out rocker, but he feels that it's commercial—and that's what singles are all about!

Miniature microphone

A miniature condenser microphone only 3 in. long by 11/16 in diameter has been introduced by Jagor Interelectric, Mercury House, Hanger Green, London, W5.

Weighing only 1⅜ oz., the

model is made in Sweden and is intended for use as a hand microphone, a lavalier microphone or a stand-mounted unit, and is available in two types—omni-directional or cardioid.

TOY INSTRUMENTS THE ONE AND ONLY

Manufacturer: UNKNOWN
Name: ELECPHONE
Date, Place: 1976, JAPAN

One optical variation for the Japanese market. Yes, these people are very special.

TOY INSTRUMENTS THE ONE AND ONLY

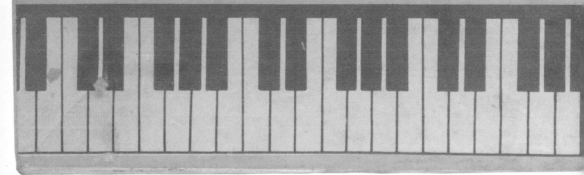

«электроника»

ИГРУШКА ЭЛЕКТРОННАЯ МУЗЫКАЛЬНАЯ

Manufacturer: UNKNOWN
Name: ELEKTRONIKA
Date, Place: 1985, USSR

If the development of musical toys represents the development of national technology, America would have never been afraid of Russian nuclear bombs. This stylophone was released when the rest of the world was going digital.

FOR GIRLS & BOYS

The Classic Toy Organ

Manufacturer: VANITY FAIR
Name: SHAUN CASSIDY ELECTRONIC ORGAN
Date, Place: 1977, HONG KONG

Who knew that this toy organ would last longer than Shaun Cassidy's celebrity.

TOY INSTRUMENTS FOR GIRLS & BOYS

Manufacturer: VANITY FAIR
Name: KAPTAIN KOOL ELECTRONIC ORGAN
Date, Place: 1977, HONG KONG

Hey Kaptain Kool, wait a minute. I have a fantastic idea. We put your name on a nonsense toy organ because it is like you: kool looking and awful sounding. What do you think? Kool?

Manufacturer: CREATIVE PLAYTHINGS
Name: LITTLE MAESTRO
Date, Place: 1977, HONG KONG

Sonic power that cracks concrete walls and crushes human ears.

TOY INSTRUMENTS FOR GIRLS & BOYS

Model Number 554

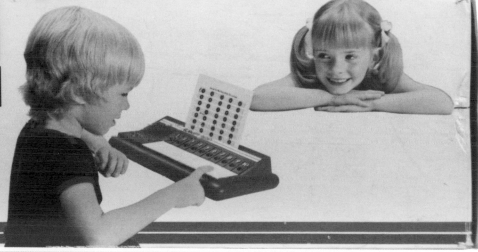

Manufacturer: CONCEPT 2000
Name: LITE'N LEARN
Date, Place: 1980, HONG KONG

The one and only: speechless (see introduction).

YOUR RHYTHM MACHINE

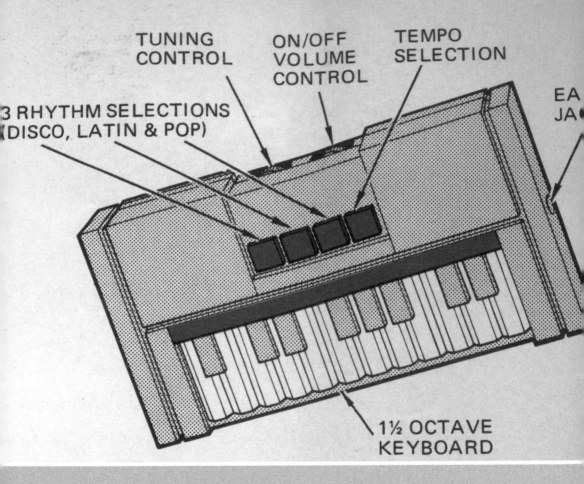

TUNING CONTROL

ON/OFF VOLUME CONTROL

TEMPO SELECTION

3 RHYTHM SELECTIONS (DISCO, LATIN & POP)

EA JA

1½ OCTAVE KEYBOARD

Manufacturer: MATTEL
Name: BEE GEES RHYTHM MACHINE
Date, Place: 1978, USA

Unfortunately the Bee Gees have never played this on any of their albums. Or were their voices three Rhythm Machines? Kraftwerk used it, and for good reason. The remarkable sound can be pitched extremely well and merge drastically with the super reduced rhythm section. This is a full noise orchestra that fits in one hand.

HAMBURGERS, LEMONS & VAMPIRES

Weird Shaped Organs

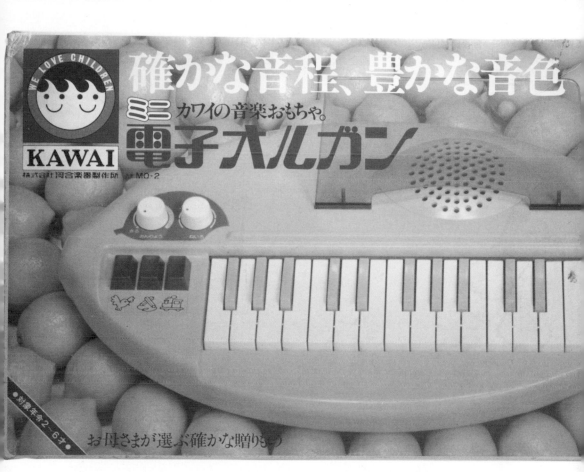

Manufacturer: KAWAI
Name: LEMON ORGAN
Date: 1977, JAPAN

It's an apple! Nooo! It's a peach! Nooo! It's SUPERLEMON!!! Yeeeah!

THE COUNT'S MUSIC MACHINE

Plays 12 pre-programmed tunes aut
many other tunes on the keyboard.
cards included.

Not recommen

FEATURES:
Automatic Play of
Manual Play allow
the keyboard.
Color Coded Musi
Make up your ow
Flip-Top Storage
No assembly requ
Uses standard 9 v
not included).

Model Number 55

THE COUNT'S MUSIC MACHINE

SESAME STREET CTW

'S*
NE

ically! Play
 coded music
r children under 3.

es.
to play tunes on

s are easy to follow.
   too!
Music Cards.

ery (battery

unt*

son's

Manufacturer: CONCEPT 2000
Name: THE COUNT'S MUSIC MACHINE
Date, Place: 1980, HONG KONG

You can only play scary tunes with this!

Burgers Organ

USE 2 "C" SIZE
(UM-2) BATTERIES
(NOT INCLUDED)

ABC SONG

HAPPY BIRTHDAY TO YOU

ROW ROW ROW YOUR BOAT

LONDON BRIDGE IS FALLING DOWN

Burgers Organ

Manufacturer: UNKNOWN
Name: BURGERS ORGAN
Date, Place: 1984, HONG KONG

Outside a burger, inside a clown. Hmmmmm...

SKATEBOARD ORGAN

For Children Over 3 Years Old

Manufacturer: UNKNOWN
Name: SKATEBOARD ORGAN
Date: 1990, HONG KONG

The wheels are the best part of this useless thing.

I AM ROBOT

Voice Changers

AGES 4 AND OVER

THE REAL GHOSTBUSTERS ™

I'LL GET YOU

GHOST SPOOKER™

VOICE MODULATOR TOY

MAKE YOUR VOICE SOUND LIKE A SCARY GHOST

I'LL GET YOU

VOLUME   PITCH   OFF

CE Kenner

CONTENTS: VOICE MODULATOR TOY WITH MICROPHONE.
REQUIRES 2 LR6 ALKALINE BATTERIES (NOT INCLUDED).

Manufacturer: KENNER
Name: GHOSTBUSTERS GHOST SPOOKER
Date: 1984, UK

For creepy nights under the sheets. Attention! This toy creates real angst.

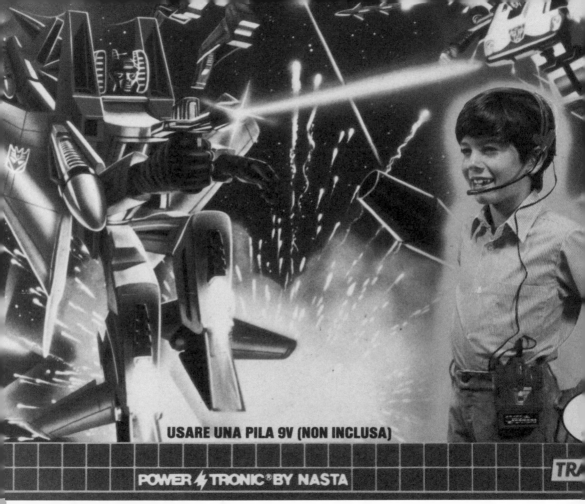

USARE UNA PILA 9V (NON INCLUSA)

POWER ⚡ TRONIC® BY NASTA

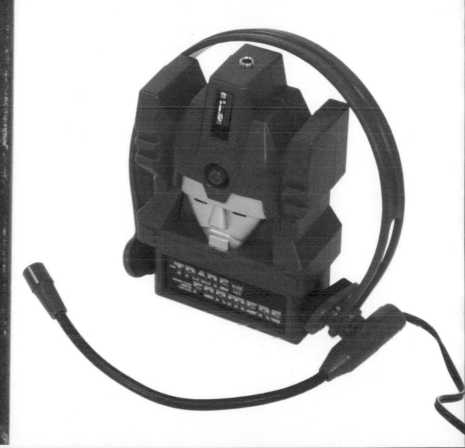

Manufacturer: NASTA
Name: ELECTRONIC VOICE TRANSFORMER
Date: 1984, HONG KONG

Your intelligence is artificial? You can transform into anything?
Take this simple tremolo-effect, produced by a cheap Hong Kong
electronic circuit, and show who you really are.

The Incredible VOICE CHANGER

◄◄◄ LOW   NORMAL   HIGH ►►►

VOL ▷ ▷▷ ▷▷▷

TOMY.

LOW

GRAVE TIEF BASSO

NORMAL

NORMAL NORMAL NORMALE

HIGH

AIGU HOCH ALTO

THE Incredible VOICE CHANGER

(III LOW   NORMAL   HIGH III)

VOL   II   III   IIII

OFF   ON

TOMY.

Manufacturer: TOMY
Name: INCREDIBLE VOICE CHANGER
Date, Place: 1988, SINGAPORE

Put the little microphone too close to the loudspeaker. Something incredible will happen.

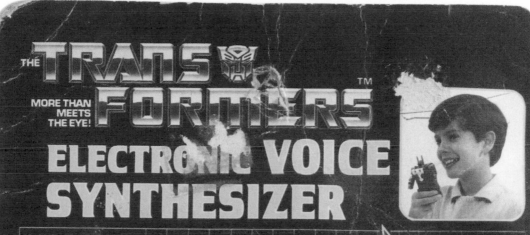

Manufacturer: NASTA
Name: TRANSFORMERS ELECTRONIC VOICE
SYNTHESIZER
Date, Place: 1986, HONG KONG

This little robot creates perfect misunderstandings with outerspace-didgeridoo-transformational noise. Believe me, even your parents won't understand you. For example: "Wooowwweeewuaaawwoowww" means: Hi Mom and Dad, I have nothing to say!

GO BOTS

MIGHTY ROBOTS
MIGHTY VEHICLES

VOICE CHANGER

YOUR VOICE SOUNDS LIKE A ROBOT'S

229 $ 5.00

Playtime

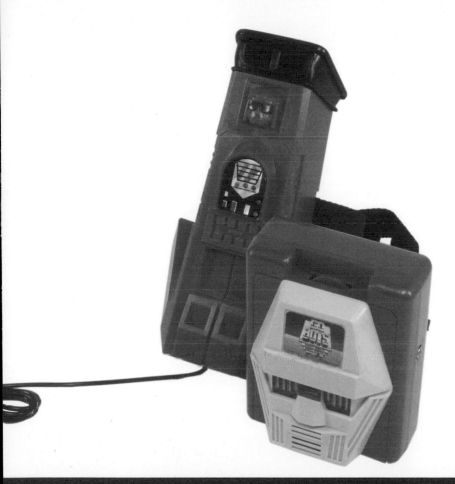

Manufacturer: PLAYTIME
Name: GO BOTS VOICE CHANGER
Date: 1985, HONG KONG

In the world of voice changers there is no class war. The poor man's excuse for a Transformer—otherwise known as a Go Bot— has the same robotic sound.

HEADACHE INLCLUDED

Noise Generators

Manufacturer: OHIO ART
Name: SKETCH-A-TUNE
Date, Place: 1975, USA

Let us remember all of the devastated children of the 1970s who tried to play nursery rhymes but failed. This machine can only sound like a garbled, battery-powered soundtrack to *One Thousand and One Nights*.

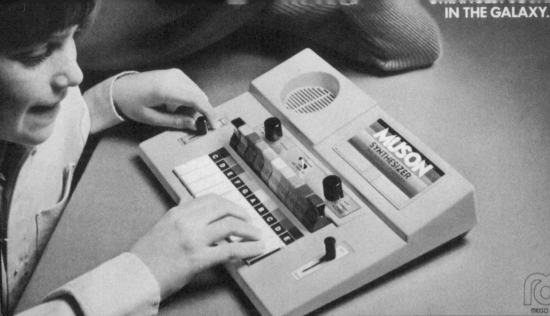

IN THE GALAXY.

NUSON SYNTHESIZER

MEGO CORP

PLAY DOZENS OF SIMPLE TUNES ON THE PIANO-TYPE KEYBOARD
OR MAKE STRANGE AND SPACEY RHYTHMS ON THE COLOR-CODED ELECTRONIC BOARD.
PLAY THEM TOGETHER FOR ROCK 'N ROLL SOUNDS, EERIE SOUNDS, OR OUTERSPACE ELECTRONIC MUSIC.
SEPARATE SLIDE LEVERS, CHANGE THE PITCH AND TEMPO. EXPERIMENT WITH THOUSANDS OF COMBINATIONS OF SOUND

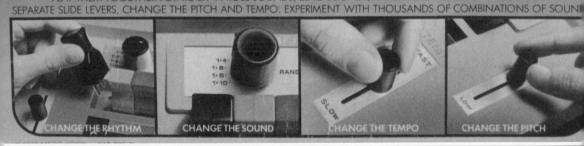

CHANGE THE RHYTHM   CHANGE THE SOUND   CHANGE THE TEMPO   CHANGE THE PITCH

TOY INSTRUMENTS HEADACHE INCLUDED

Manufacturer: MEGO
Name: MUSON SYNTHESIZER
Date, Place: 1978, TAIWAN

With just ten colored plugs and two flexible sliders you'll start a psychedelic trip without any drugs. I think the lucky kids who called this rare toy their own are now all members of Muson Anonymous.

TOY INSTRUMENTS HEADACHE INCLUDED

Manufacturer: REMCO
Name: SOUND FX MACHINE
Date, Place: 1978, TAIWAN

Use the many knobs carefully, because some brains can't handle listening to the sound of spiritual aliens, dysfunctional space guns and enlightened scientists.

TOY INSTRUMENTS HEADACHE INCLUDED

Manufacturer: BANDAI
Name: KINNIKUMAN ANNOUNCER
Date: 1984, JAPAN

Whatever the intention of this thing was, it failed. You can't understand any word recorded onto its magnetic cards. Maybe the Japanese designers wanted to be the real pioneers of scratching?

OFF

SURF I

SURF II

RAIN

WATERFALL

SELECTOR

SLOW   FAST

SURF RATE

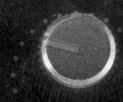

BASS   TREBLE

TONE

))))))**MARSONA**®

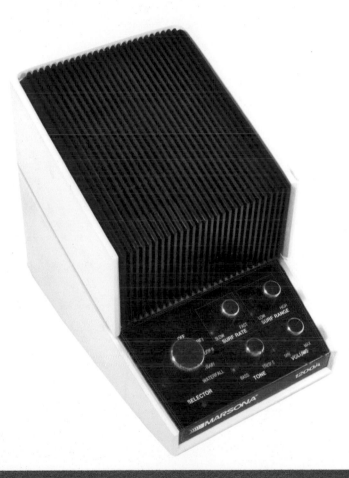

Manufacturer: MARSONA
Name: SOUND CONDITIONER
Date: 1986, USA

Made for relaxation, this heavy machine fills the air with brutal white noise.

DARLING, IT'S PLAYTIME!

Musical Games

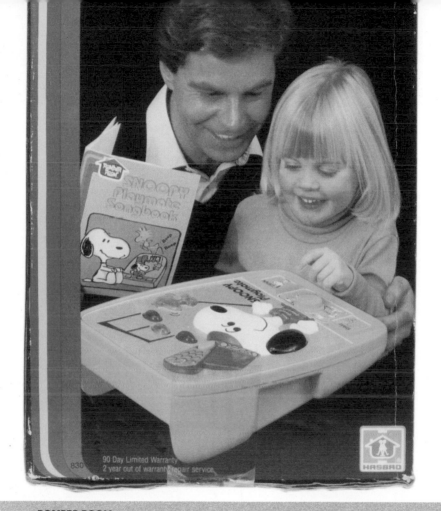

Manufacturer: ROMPER ROOM
Name: SNOOPY PLAYMATE
Date, Place: 1980, USA

Man, this is big.

TOY INSTRUMENTS DARLING, IT'S PLAYTIME!

Manufacturer: KINGSFORD
Name: MINI MATCH ME
Date, Place: 1980, USA

For mom and dad it's a Brain-Trainer. For boys and girls it's a Disco-Organ. For me it's a Time-Killer.

TOY INSTRUMENTS DARLING, IT'S PLAYTIME!

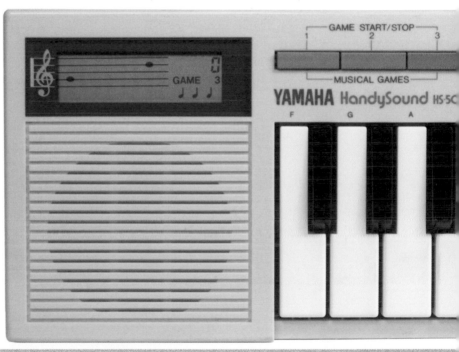

Manufacturer: YAMAHA
Name: HANDYSOUND HS-501
Date, Place: 1982, JAPAN

Instead of killing aliens like in *Space Invaders* you have to hit little
attacking notes. I don't know any other toy keyboard with such a
destructive feature.

TOY INSTRUMENTS DARLING, IT'S PLAYTIME!

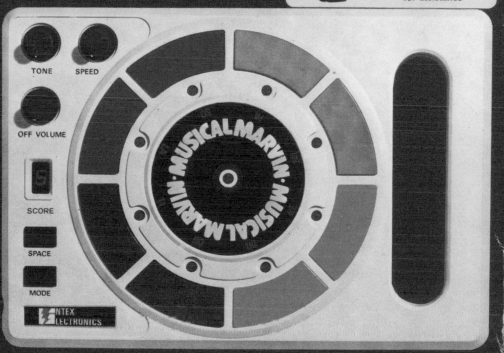

TONE SPEED

OFF VOLUME

MUSICAL MARVIN · MUSICAL MARVIN · MUSICAL

S
SCORE

SPACE

MODE

ENTEX
LECTRONICS

1 to 4 playe
their skill ag
Marvin,™ a
game mach
6 musical g
iable speed
tone contro
excitement
play Marvin
full-octave
ment. It car
and play ba
musical cor

☐ It's an 8-n
☐ It plays 6
musical g
☐ It record
back—yo
composi
☐ For 1 to 4
☐ Variable
skill cont
☐ Volume c
☐ Tone con
☐ Automati
scoreboa
☐ AC adapt
jack
☐ Ages 5
to adult

☐ It's an 8-note organ ☐ It plays 6 different musical games
☐ It records—and plays back—your musical compositions ☐ For 1 to 4 players

USES 6 "AA" BATTERIES, NOT INCLUDED

Manufacturer: ENTEX
Name: MUSICAL MARVIN
Date: 1980, TAIWAN

I can hear the creative director talking to his team: "Three knobs,
I want three ultra-cool looking knobs. They don't need to be really
functional or useful. Just three knobs. Do you understand?"

1+1=BEEP

Musical Calculators

eingestellt: Musikredakteur Manfred Gillig (links). Franz-Peter Strohbücker, Ressortleiter Magazin.

Manufacturer: CASIO
Name: VL-TONE VL-1
Date, Place: 1980, JAPAN

Holy Miniorgan! How many people really understood the so-called ADSR function? And how many people were able to play these small keys?

You've heard it? Now play it!
Play any tune you like with just one finger.
No special training or talent needed.

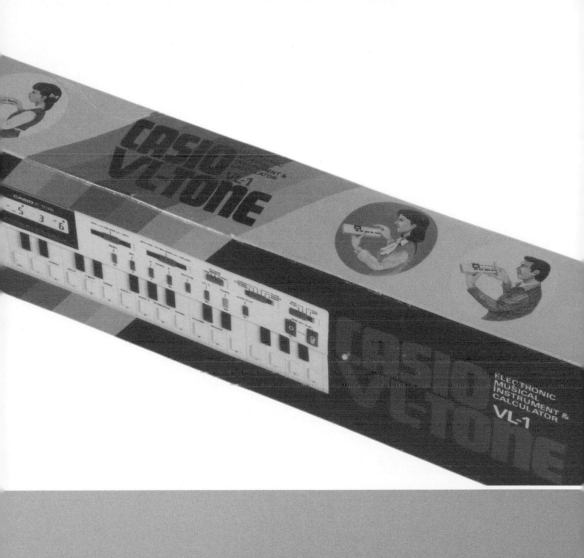

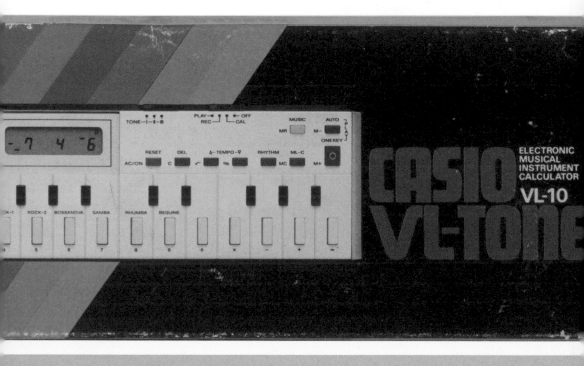

TOY INSTRUMENTS 1+1= BEEP

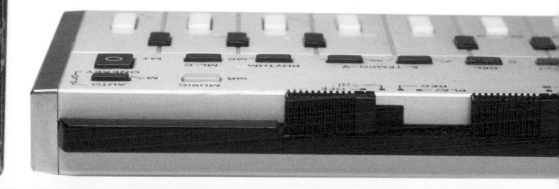

Manufacturer: CASIO
Name: VL-TONE VL-10
Date, Place: 1981, JAPAN

Here comes the advanced version of the VL-1 for adults who have fingers like babies. Feel the cool aluminium in your hand and discover the ingenuity of two separate loudspeakers—one for the melody, one for the rhythm. Just call it state-of-the-80s-art.

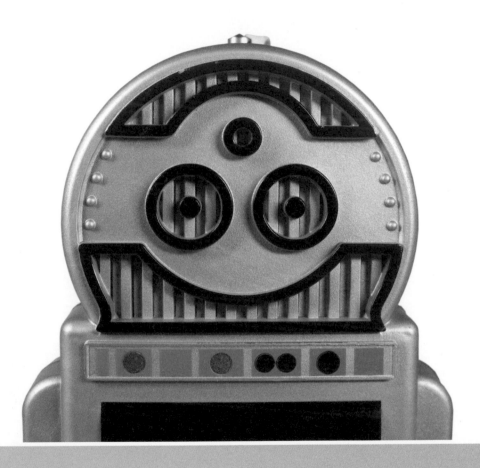

TOY INSTRUMENTS 1+1= BEEP

MR. MUS-I-CAL

It's a musical math teaching machine!
It's a four-function calculator!
It's a real musical instrument!

MUSICAL MATH TEACHING MACHINE

Enter a problem in addition, subtraction, multiplication or division—and punch in your answer—if you're correct, MR. MUS-I-CAL will actually play "The Stars and Stripes Forever"! But if your answer is wrong—it will play "The Funeral March" and you must try again.

FOUR-FUNCTION CALCULATOR

Add, subtract, divide and multiply!
A handy tool for home, school or anywhere.

PLAY MUSIC

Manufacturer: CONCEPT 2000
Name: MR. MUS-I-CAL
Date, Place: 1979, HONG KONG

Wonderful little robot with a musical attitude and scary smile.

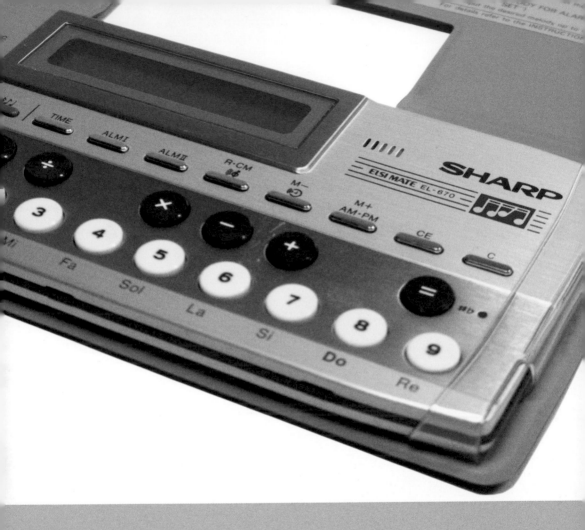

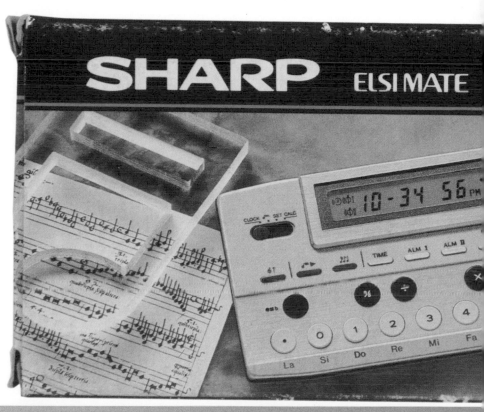

Manufacturer: SHARP
Name: ELSI MATE EL-670
Date, Place: 1982, JAPAN

Yuppies were drawn to this silver streamlined design in a leather case. It also features an alarm clock that plays a melody of your own creation so you won't miss any important meetings, whether with your boss or drug dealer.

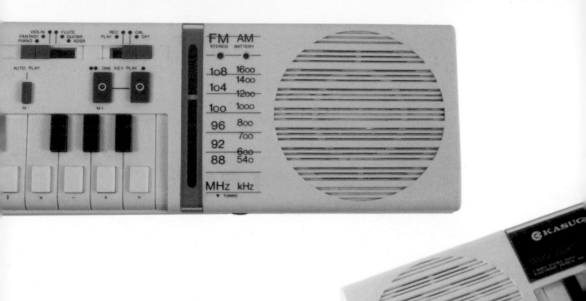

TOY INSTRUMENTS 1+1= BEEP

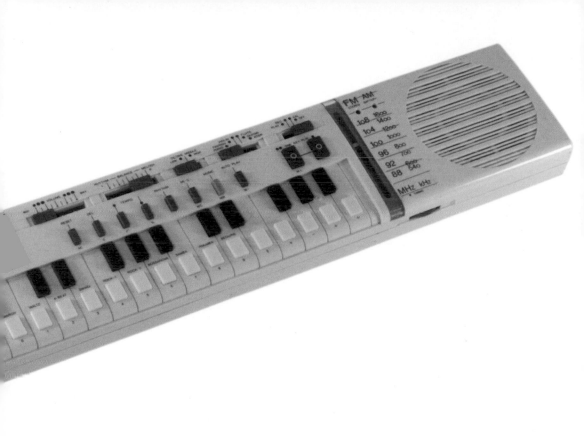

Manufacturer: KAZUGA
Name: KR-7
Date: UNKNOWN, TAIWAN

A bizarre variation of the famous Casio VL-1. Calculator, rhythm machine, sequencer and synthesizer weren't enough. A radio had to be included to make this manly toy reeeeeeally long.

33 RPM
FOR BEGINNERS

Turntables

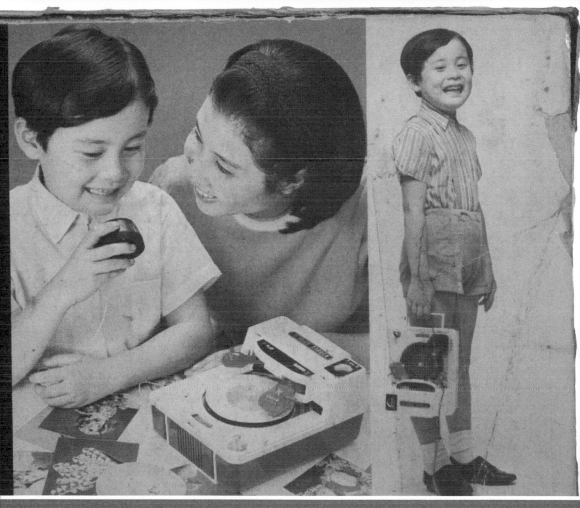

Manufacturer: TOMY
Name: VOICE CORDER
Date, Place: 1972, JAPAN

Even futuristic Japan was not ready for this fantastic machine that cuts dub-plates! Yes, you read right—cutting your own vinyl! This special toy was maybe made for super-rich Japanese kids, but the market was not big enough. And then tape-recorders made this outstanding concept obsolete.

TOY INSTRUMENTS 33 RPM FOR BEGINNERS

do * re * mi

OPERATED PRODUCT
Not recommended for children under
4 years of age. As with all electric
products, precautions should be
observed during handling and use
to prevent electric shock. AC/Bat-
tery operated. 120 V., 60 Hz only,
6 Watts.

SG-123

　　TOY INSTRUMENTS 33 RPM FOR BEGINNERS

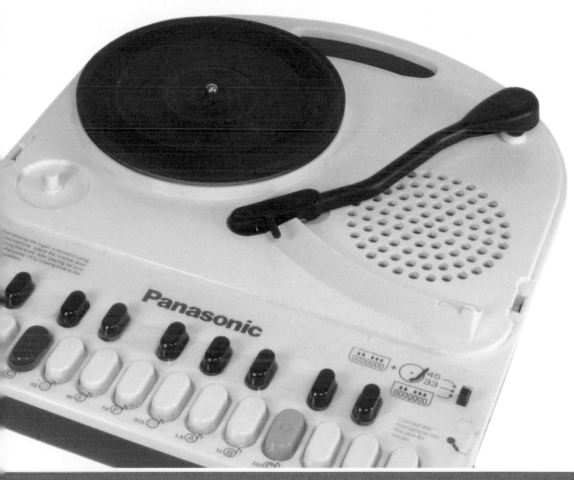

Manufacturer: PANASONIC
Name: DO RE MI SG-123
Date, Place: 1977, JAPAN

Just visionary: listen to your favorite tune, sing like a little bird and be loved by the best mother on earth, all because she bought you this huge hunk of electronic plastic.

TOY INSTRUMENTS 33 RPM FOR BEGINNERS

★ふたをしめれば
★マイクでうたっ
★人形がおどる

Manufacturer: KENNER
Name: DANCING PLAYER
Date, Place: 1978, JAPAN

Oh, a dancing pop group. They move to the beat and they rattle to the sound. Imagine playing some death metal....

MINI, MICRO, NANO

Smallest Organs

Manufacturer: UNKNOWN
Name: SAILOR MOON MINI PIANO
Date: 1993, TAIWAN

The *Sailor Moon* girls have superpowers to save the world from evil. But they forgot to save the world from useless toys.

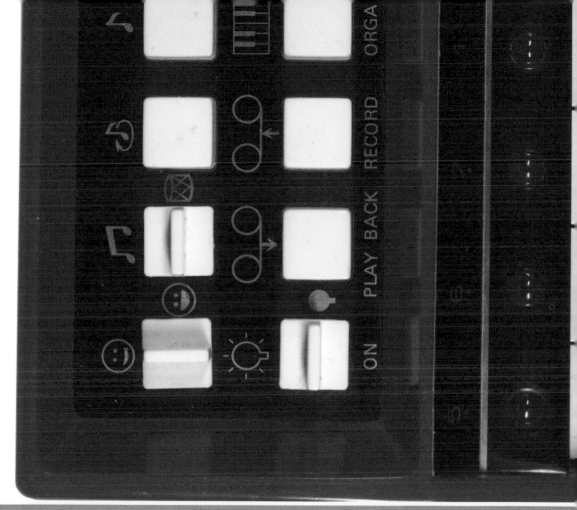

Manufacturer: ALLIED
Name: MICOM ORGAN
Date, Place: 1980, HONG KONG

The sales copy goes big: "Make sweet dreams come true by technic—for Baby, Child, Mom and Dad." In reality this is one of the worst sounding but best shaped organs I have ever seen.

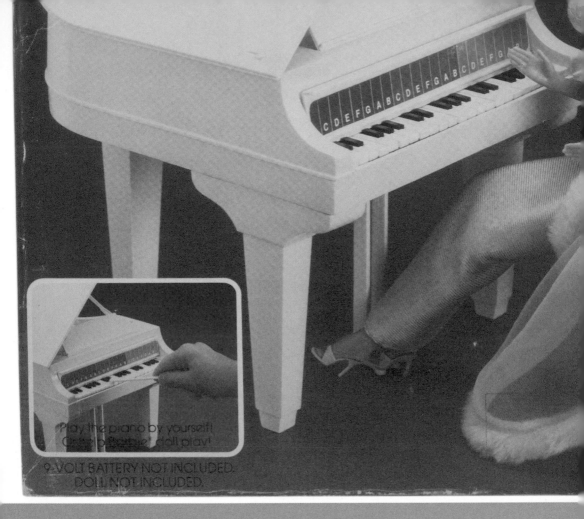

"Play the piano by yourself!
Or help 'Barbie' doll play!"

9-VOLT BATTERY NOT INCLUDED.
DOLL NOT INCLUDED.

Manufacturer: MATTEL
Name: BARBIE ELECTRONIC PIANO
Date: 1981, USA

My daughter always wanted to have this piano, but she learned quickly that it is impossible to "play" because these are definitely the smallest keys I have ever seen. Even the enclosed stick doesn't make it better. So, like many other Barbie toys, this is more decoration than inspiration. Boys view, sure!

MUSIX GRAPHIX

Vetrex Musical Software & Hardware

Manufacturer: GCE
Name: VECTREX MELDODY MASTER
Date, Place: 1982, USA

It looks very futuristic to sit in a shaded room with your white glowing face in front of the Vectrex—the most famous retrogame machine nowadays. With special Melody Master and Light Pen software you can create your own drum and melody sequences live on screen.

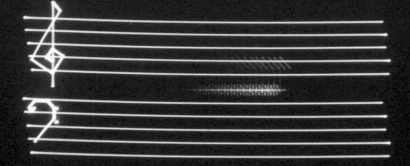

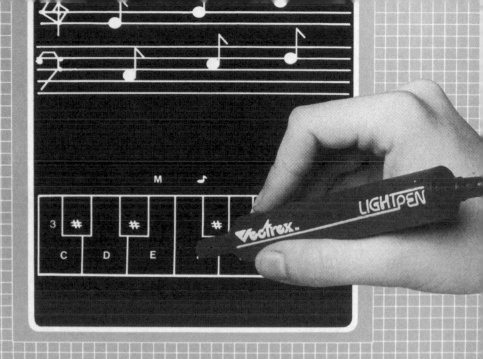

TOUCH ME, BABY!

Foil Key Organs

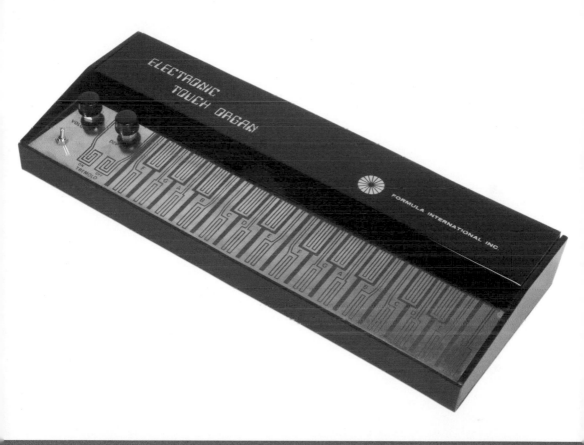

Manufacturer: FORMULA
Name: ELECTRONIC TOUCH ORGAN
Date, Place: 1977, USA

With dry hands you create weird microtonal tunes, but with wet hands you get the full sounds. So this machine can really read your emotions. Maybe useful as a lie-detector.

TOY INSTRUMENTS TOUCH ME, BABY!

ompute-a-tune

10 musical effects & music teaching memory

replays notes or tunes from the tune memory at four selectable

to follow & learn
2. Normal Tempo - slow
4. Fast Tempo - for use with chord & echo effects

notes or tune stored in the tune memory

Y - completely clears the tune memory ready for new notes to

ices in place of notes into the tune memory to give replayed

ses the last note played on the keyboard from the tune memory.

Hi Fi system

HUL introduces exciting note mixing effects.

ROL

(2) **NOTE SWITCH** - selects played and re-played note effects.
NORMAL without added effects
ECHO adds echo effect
CHORD adds sequential chord effect

(3) **TUNE SWITCH** - selects one of four tunes from COMPUTE A TUNES permanent memory, to start learning from.

(4) **ON OFF** switch

compute-a-tune
effects — volume

(12) **KEYBOARD TUNING**

(13) **TWO OCTAVE** tunable monophonic keyboard allowing accompaniment of other musical instruments

---

○ ERS AND REPLAYS 32 NOTES
○ AND EFFECTS CONTROLS
○ O EASY TO LEARN TUNES

○ FOUR BUILT IN TUNES TO LEARN FROM
○ TWO OCTAVE TUNEABLE KEYBOARD
○ CHORD AND ECHO EFFECTS

Manufacturer: WADDINGTONS
Name: COMPUTE-A-TUNE
Date, Place: 1978, UK

Oh, I want to be back in the Space Age. I want to listen to echo effects and a pseudo filter function 24 hours a day. I want to compute a tune.

POOU !

おしりでもOK!

世界中と合わせて！

内容：ドレミマジック（9V乾電池使用、電

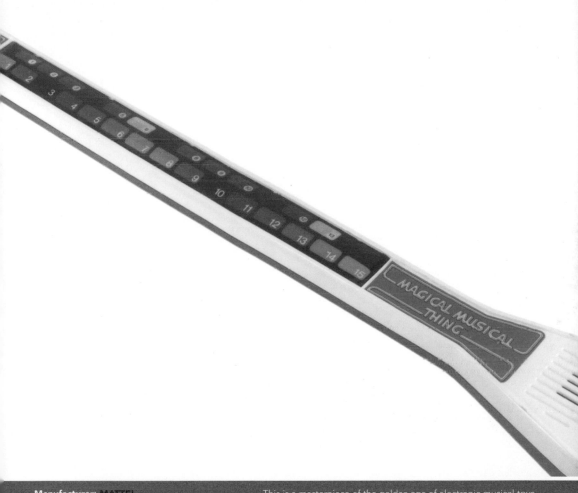

Manufacturer: MATTEL
Name: MAGICAL MUSICAL THING
Date, Place: 1978, USA

This is a masterpiece of the golden age of electronic musical toys. Imagine the possible ways of playing this detuned thing. Just send me a sketch of your way of playing.

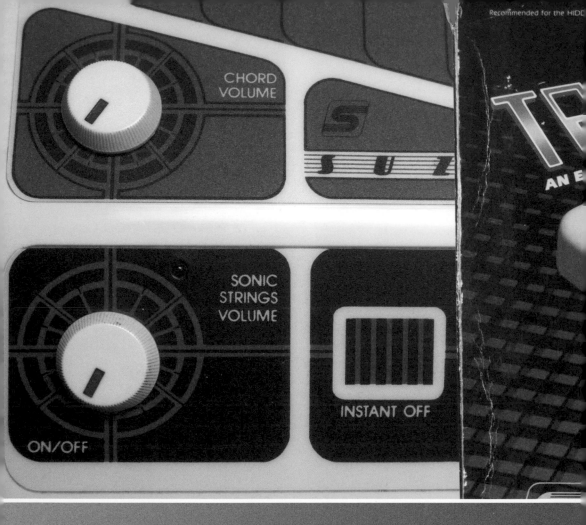

CHORD
VOLUME

SONIC
STRINGS
VOLUME

ON/OFF

INSTANT OFF

TOY INSTRUMENTS TOUCH ME, BABY!

Manufacturer: SUZUKI
Name: TRONICHORD
Date, Place: 1980, JAPAN

You'll forget time and space when you play the Tronichord. The sound and the chords are not from earth. It makes me see angels, drifting through space, touching the stars and bringing the light. Just with one finger.

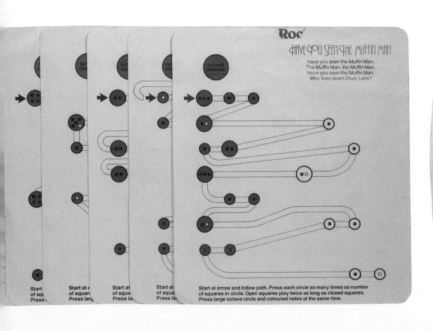

HAVE YOU SEEN THE MUFFIN MAN

Have you seen the Muffin Man,
The Muffin Man, the Muffin Man,
Have you seen the Muffin Man,
Who lives down Drury Lane?

OCTAVE CHANGE

Start at arrow and follow path. Press each circle as many times as number of squares in circle. Open squares play twice as long as closed squares. Press large octave circle and coloured notes at the same time.

Start at a
of squa
Press la

Start at
of squa
Press la

Start at
of squa
Press la

Start at
of squ
Press

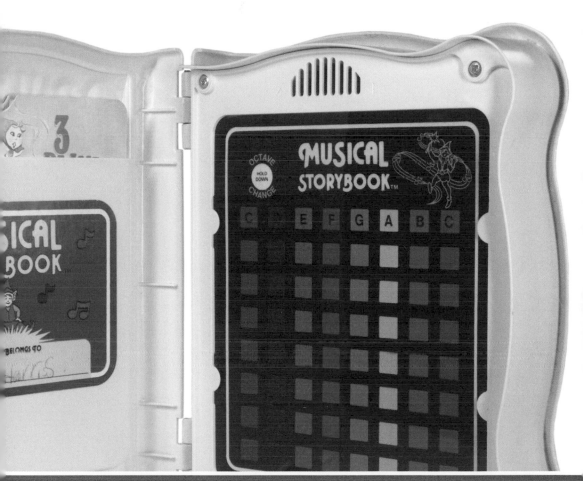

Manufacturer: **OHIO ART**
Name: **PETER PAN MUSICAL STORYBOOK**
Date, Place: **1981, USA**

Sixty-four keys offer a new and innovative way of composing. Play the "Magic Touch Keyboard" wild and untamed. You'll get the highest praise from the abstract-electronica-scene.

LISTEN TO THE TIME!

Musical Watches

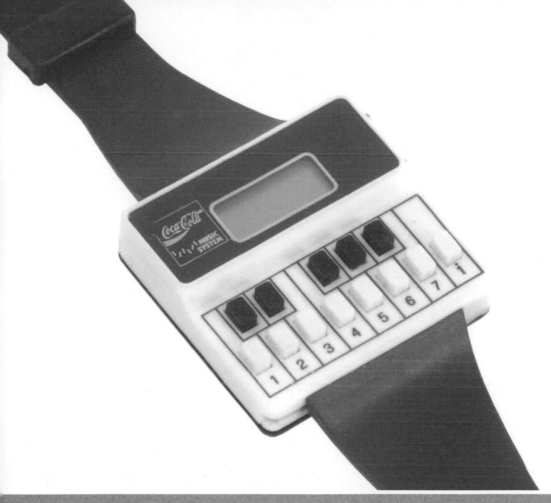

Manufacturer: UNKNOWN
Name: COCA COLA MUSIC SYSTEM
Date, Place: UNKNOWN, HONG KONG

What a big promise. Maybe I haven't checked all the functions of this so called "Music System."

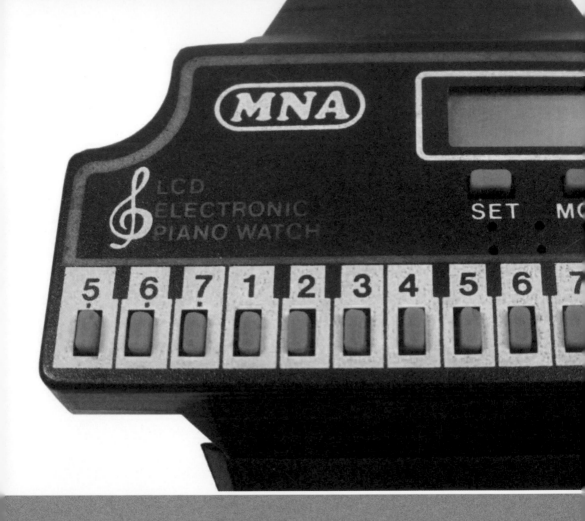

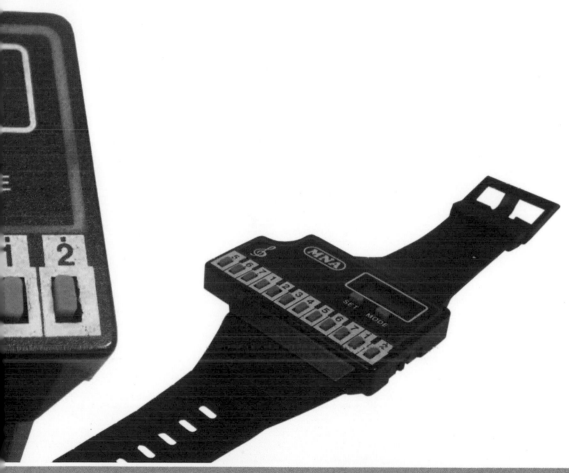

Manufacturer: MNA
Name: PIANO WATCH
Date, Place: Unknown, HONG KONG

You don't have money for wristwatches from Swiss watchmakers such as Patek Philippe, Vacheron Constantin, Girard-Perregaux and the like? Take this MNA one. Potential love interests will be very impressed.

Manufacturer: UNKNOWN
Name: ECHO 500
Date: Unknown, HONG KONG

I don't hear an echo. I don't even hear 500 echos! Did I do something wrong?

OH, KARAOKE

Sing-A-Longs

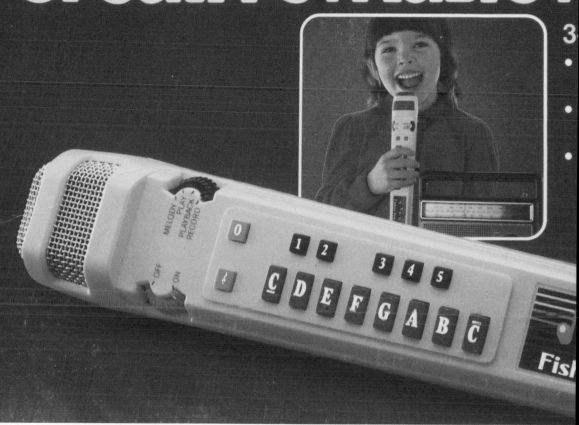

Creative Music

Manufacturer: **FISHER PRICE**
Name: **CREATIVE MUSIC MAKER**
Date, Place: **1986, HONG KONG**

I cannot imagine a four-year-old child able to play and sing at the same time. Another great technical failure that is highly collectible.

ピンク・レディー
おしゃれ マイク

Manufacturer: UNKNOWN
Name: PINK LADY MAIKU
Date, Place: 1977, JAPAN

Pink Lady was a very famous Japanese pop group and they released tons of audio trash and plastic merchandising. This little amp was made for all the Japanese Pink Ladies who thought they could sing.

さあ！
ステージオンマイクで
あなたもスター!!
キャンティーズと
いっしょに
うたいましょう！

マイク
スタンド付ョ！

Manufacturer: BANDAI
Name: CANDIES MAIKU
Date, Place: 1978, JAPAN

Just another girlie band from Japan. But the third voice doesn't make it better.

TOY INSTRUMENTS OH, KARAOKE

Manufacturer: POPY
Name: CANDY CANDY
Date, Place: 1980, JAPAN

Sorry if you are depressed and have suicidal tendencies, but this is only made for happy children with a happy family.

©1982, 1984 SANRIO CO., LTD.

006P 乾電池付

Manufacturer: TAKARA
Name: GOROPIKADON
Date, Place: 1983, JAPAN

Goropikadon are three cheeky brothers from the land of thunder.
Goro loves to eat and make jokes. Pika is thoughtful, shy and
good at the thunder drums. Don is serious and loves inventing
things. Amazing what a simple loudspeaker can do.

Manufacturer: QVC
Name: SCHROEDER PIANO
Date, Place: 1984, USA

The motor for the moveable figures is louder than the keyboard.
Play it for about 30 seconds for the best headache of your life!

volume

Manufacturer: LJN
Name: MICHAEL JACKSON SOUND MACHINE
Date, Place: 1984, HONG KONG

Is the girl on the box singing "Thriller" or trying to talk to MJ?
Think he's moonwalking in his grave?

NERDS WELCOME

Musical Kits

STEP-BY-STEP INSTRUCTIONS

EASILY ASSEMBLED CIRCUIT

MUSIC INCLUDE

1 OCTAVE OF MUSIC

EAR-PHONE FOR PRIVATE LISTENING

EACH KIT LOCKS WITH

Manufacturer: EMCO
Name: ADD-VENTURE KIT
Date, Place: 1975, USA

Boys and girls, just let us make a better world full of radios, amplifiers, lie-detectors, light-pens and miniorgans.

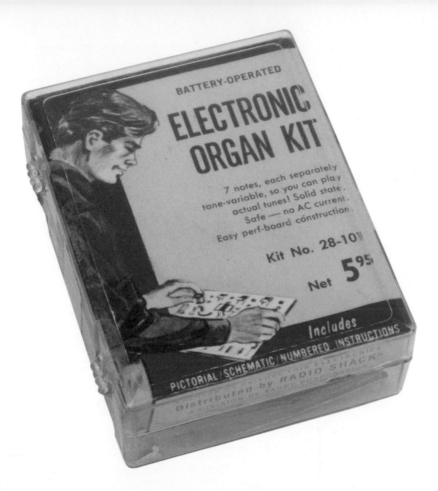

BATTERY-OPERATED

ELECTRONIC ORGAN KIT

7 notes, each separately
tone-variable, so you can play
actual tunes! Solid state.
Safe — no AC current.
Easy perf-board construction.

Kit No. 28-1011

Net **5**⁹⁵

Includes

PICTORIAL/SCHEMATIC/NUMBERED INSTRUCTIONS

Distributed by RADIO SHACK
A DIVISION OF TANDY CORPORATION

Manufacturer: SCIENCE FAIR
Name: ELECTRONIC ORGAN KIT
Date, Place: 1973, USA

Old and dirty.

Manufacturer: SHARP
Name: MZ-40 K
Date, Place: 1978, JAPAN

Technology overkill. This state-of-the-art kit offered the most complicated way to program your merrie melodies. To avoid total confusion, Sharp offered an additional rough-designed keyboard.

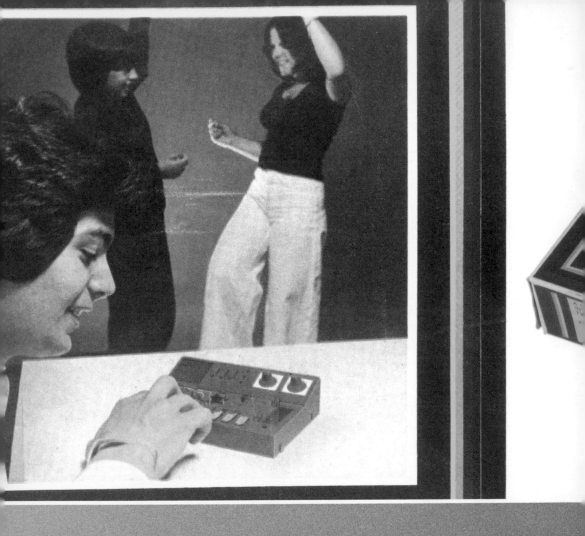

TOY INSTRUMENTS NERDS WELCOME

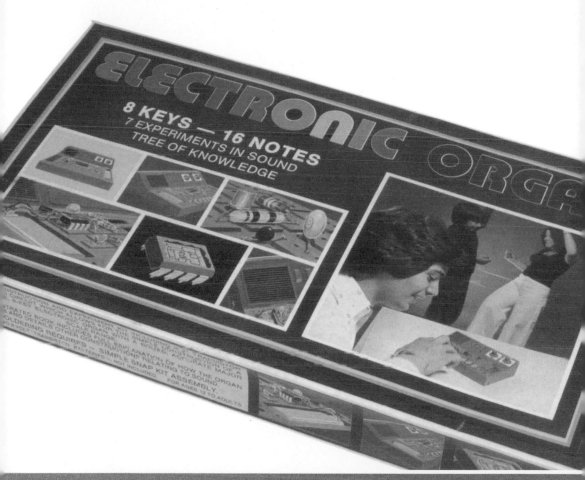

Manufacturer: TREE OF KNOWLEDGE
Name: ELECTRONIC ORGAN KIT
Date, Place: 1977, HONG KONG

I will spend two hours building this organ but you will dance for only two seconds to the sound. I think this is a fair exchange.

HIT ME

Rhythm Machines & Toy Drums

Manufacturer: KNIGHT
Name: ELECTRONIC BONGOS
Date, Place: 1966, USA

Express yourself playing these Bongos.

Manufacturer: MATTEL
Name: SYNSONICS DRUMS STEREO PRO
Date, Place: 1982, USA

Zzzzsh, boip, pffffft—I cannot describe the sound better than that. And this is the professional version!

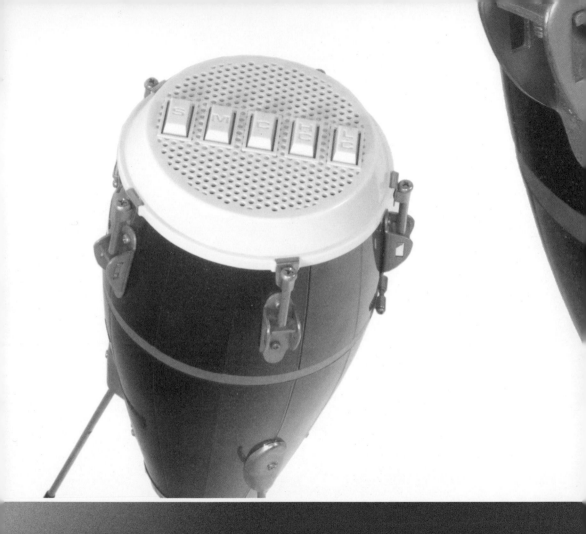

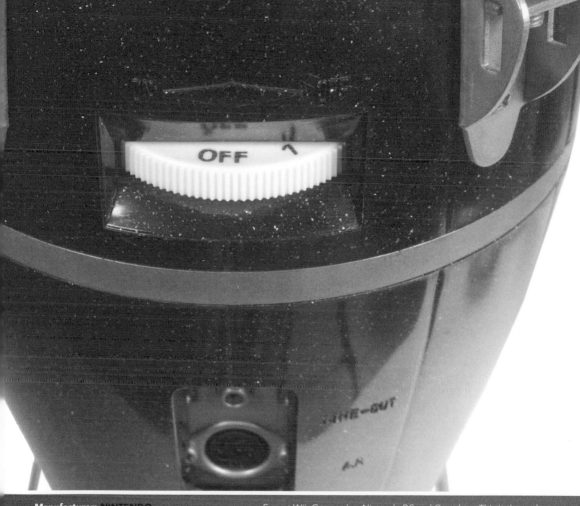

Manufacturer: NINTENDO
Name: ELECONGA
Date, Place: 1973, JAPAN

Forget Wii, Gamecube, Nintendo DS and Gameboy. This is the real deal. When Japan was wild for all things Latin, this monstrous thing came to the market. It failed. Nowadays, strange people are looking for this highly collectible item. Most of them are not Latinos.

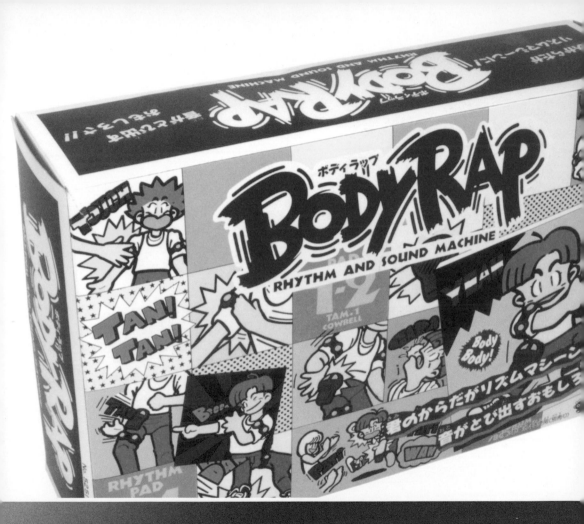

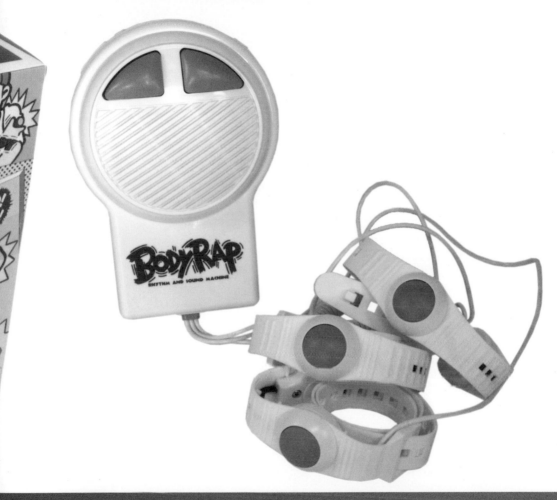

Manufacturer: TAKARA
Name: BODY RAP
Date, Place: 1984, JAPAN

Move your body and activate short rhythmic samples: Rap, Rap, Body, Body, Uh, Uh…Any more questions?

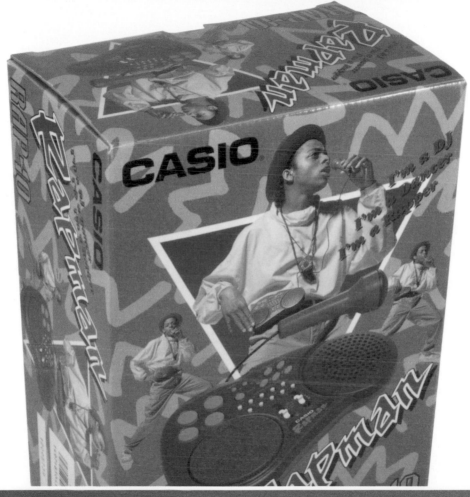

Manufacturer: CASIO
Name: RAPMAN RAP-10
Date, Place: Unknown, JAPAN

The scratch-feeling is realistic, but it looks so deformed. Why were the early 90s so ugly?

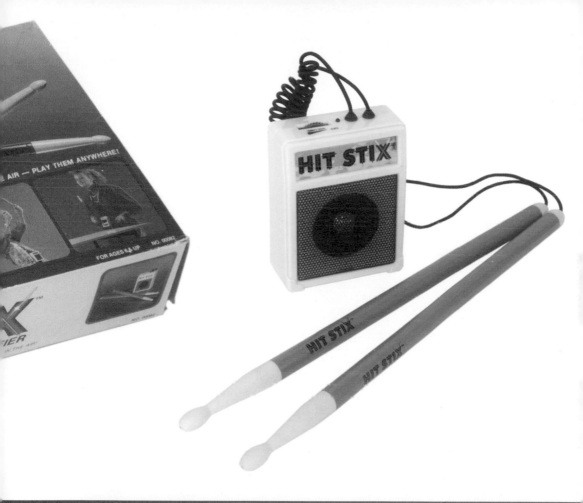

Manufacturer: NASTA
Name: HIT STIX
Date, Place: 1986, HONG KONG

It's so easy to make a hit. Just shake your arms with the Stix and you get a top-ten white noise. Bitchin' gloves not included.

ALL IN ONE

Multifunctional Organs

Manufacturer: SILVER STAR
Name: ORP-1803
Date, Place: 1976, USA

I would call it Disco-Entertainment-Center with all of these features and colors. I think this a perfect prototype of modern mobile phones. Just made for playing with everything.

TOY INSTRUMENTS ALL IN ONE

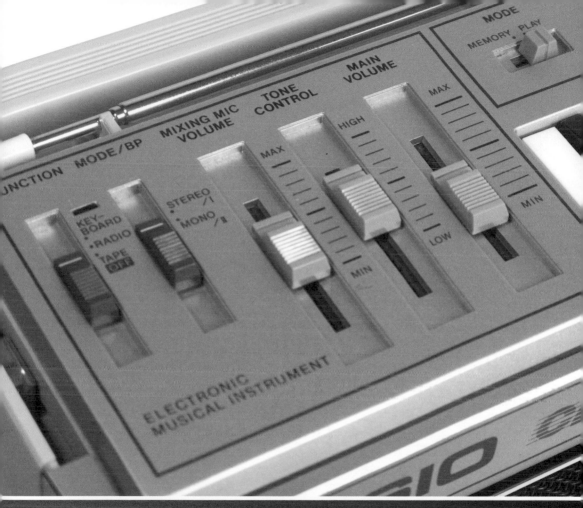

Manufacturer: CASIO
Name: CK-200
Date, Place: 1984, JAPAN

Dream of being in the 80s, walking through the streets, listening to rap music and playing that cheap violin-sound. Millions of fans will surround you.

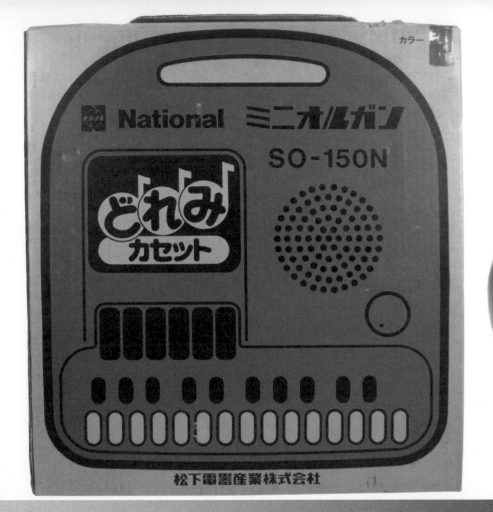

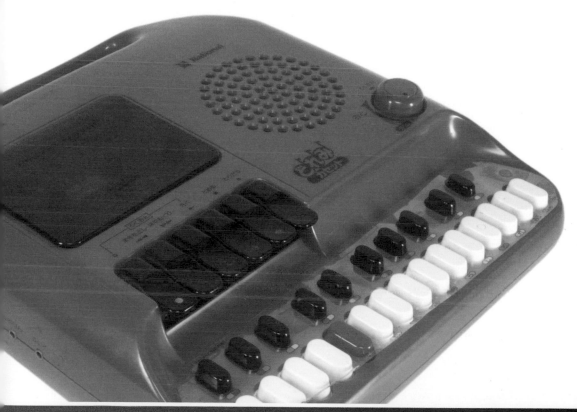

Manufacturer: NATIONAL
Name: DO RE MI SO - 150N
Date, Place: 1993, JAPAN

Very red. Very cool. Very heartbreak.

SOOO CUUUTE

Musical Animals

Manufacturer: HOURTRONIC
Name: HEATHCLIFF TUNES
Date, Place: 1984, USA

Looks like Heathcliff is trying to do more than play a tune—meow!

REAL ELECTRIC PIANO

TUNETOWN USA

America's Toy Music Maker

Jim Henson's MUPPET BABIES

ELECTRONIC PIAN

Manufacturer: TUNETOWN USA
Name: MUPPET BABIES ELECTRONIC PIANO
Date, Place: 1984, USA

There are days when I wish I had never started collecting musical toys.

TOY INSTRUMENTS SOOO CUUUTE

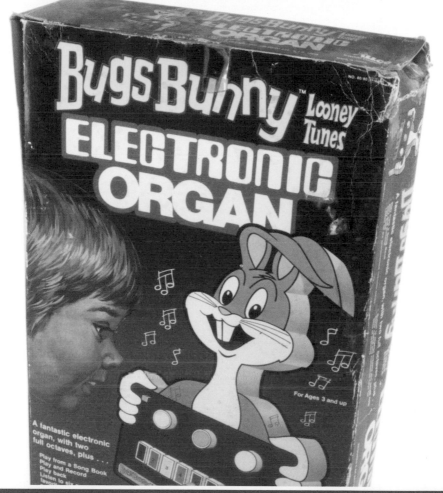

Manufacturer: ILLCO
Name: BUGS BUNNY ELECTRONIC ORGAN
Date, Place: 1980, USA

Eh, what's up, Doc?

A JOURNEY INTO SOUND

Musical Trains

メロディマイコン

コンポッポ、マイコンどうぶつ　共通説明書

世界の子供たちのために　マスダヤ

Manufacturer: MASUDAYA
Name: MICON PO PO
Date, Place: 1980, JAPAN

Have you ever tried to play a keyboard while it's driving? Some call it a true challenge. I call it pure frustration.

マイコンポッポ

メロディを 聞いたり……弾いたり……録音したり
遊びながらオルガン教室。

blank.

have completed the
ntly place the
ain on the track so
run clockwise—the
hown by the arrow
ut. Be sure that all
eels rest on the rails.
ON/OFF switch to
sition and the train
around the track and
song.

want to change
ply repeat the above
, following one of
ong diagrams.

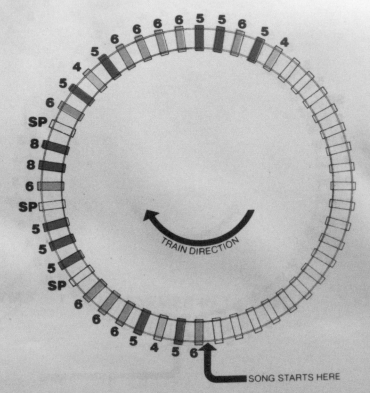

MARY HAD A LITTLE LAMB

TRAIN DIRECTION

SONG STARTS HERE

C	6	A
D	7	B
E	8	C
F	9	D
G	10	E

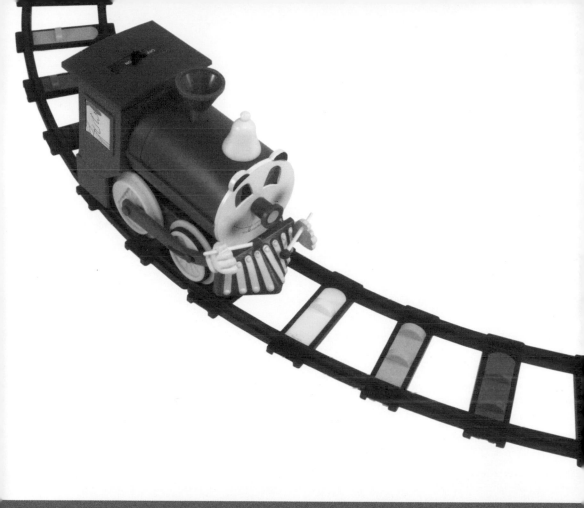

Manufacturer: CONCEPT 2000
Name: MUSICAL TRAIN
Date, Place: 1980, HONG KONG

This musical train is an analog step sequencer for 3-year-old children. No surprise that it failed like many other innovative musical toys: too complicated for youngsters.

LA SI DO MI LA

Singing & Talking Keyboards

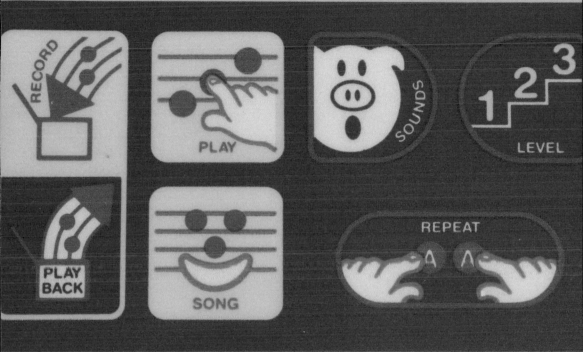

Manufacturer: TEXAS INSTRUMENTS
Name: LITTLE MAESTRO
Date, Place: 1986, USA

It has a pig sound. It has a pig sound. It has a pig sound. Make it squeal like a pig.

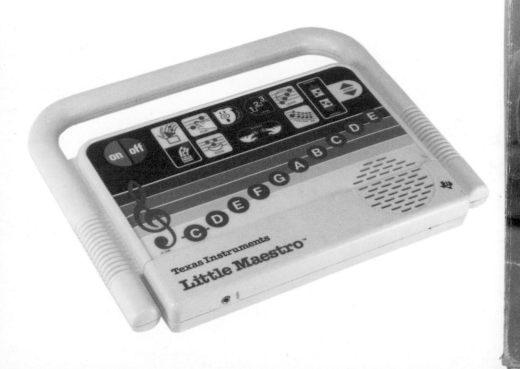

SECRET   SAY
CODE   LETTER   IT   SPELL

🔑   ??   😃   ON

G   H   I   J

Q   R   S   T

Manufacturer: TEXAS INSTRUMENTS
Name: SPEAK & SPELL
Date, Place: 1985, USA

Dad is always at work? Or not home for "other reasons?" Don't be sad. Here's a little orange machine with a deep, manly voice saying: "Good."

ROCK STAR MANIA

Guitars & Violins

kids!

Manufacturer: MATTEL
Name: STARMAKER GUITAR
Date, Place: 1980, USA

Motörhead is nothing compared to the greatest toy guitar on earth. It creates the most brutal feedback noise you can imagine—without using any additional gear. Just take it in your hands and demolish walls with the sound of this unearthly plastic axe.

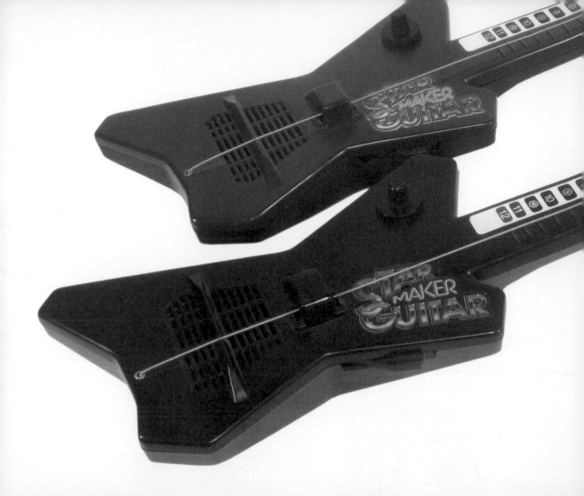

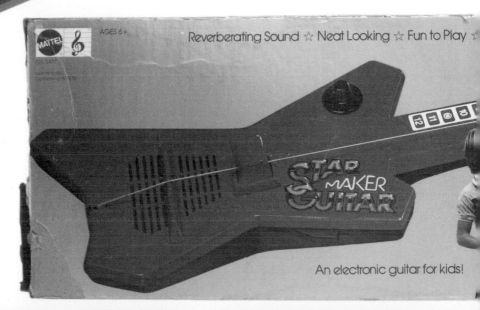

TOY INSTRUMENTS ROCK STAR MANIA

Manufacturer: TYCO
Name: HOT KEYZ
Date, Place: 1990, USA

Wow, wah, whoo. Chorus, distortion, loops. You'll whip a stadium of people into a rage. And don't forget the early 90s mullet.

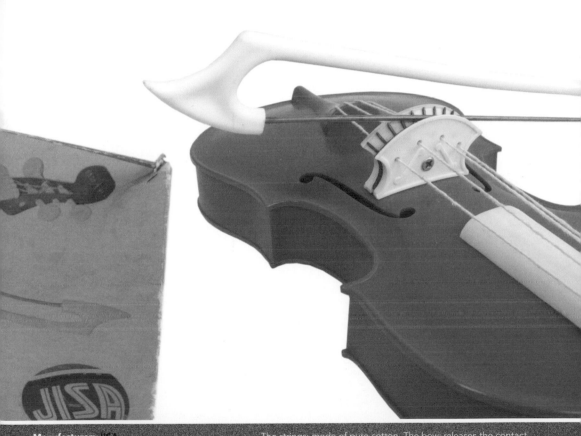

Manufacturer: JISA
Name: VIOLIN ELECTRONICO
Date, Place: UNKNOWN, MEXICO

The strings: made of pure cotton. The bow: releases the contact in the electric circuit. The result: something between Karlheinz Stockhausen and John Cage.

Toy Instruments:
Design, Nostalgia, Music
© Eric Schneider

"Serious Play" © Paul D. Miller aka DJ Spooky
Design: Carolyn Frisch

Typefaces used: Avenir, Breakaway, illD

Library of Congress Control Number: 2009933495

Printed and bound in China through Asia Pacific Offset

10 9 8 7 6 5 4 3 2 1   First Edition

This edition © 2010

Mark Batty Publisher, LLC
36 West 37th Street, Suite 409
New York, NY 10018, USA.
Email: info@MarkBattyPublisher.com
www.markbattypublisher.com

ISBN: 978-0-9820754-8-7

Distributed outside North America by:

Thames & Hudson Ltd.
181A High Holborn
London WC1V 7QX
United Kingdon
Tel: 00 44 20 7845 5000
Fax: 00 44 20 7845 5055
www.thameshudson.co.uk